It's All About

The Journey...

Dora Mar

Dora Mar Books
www.doramarbooks.com

It's All About The Journey...

Published 2008 by Dora Mar Books

www.doramarbooks.com

Cover design and photos by Robert Gromadzki

First Edition, 2008

Printed in the United States of America

ISBN 978-0-6152-4072-5

Dedication

This book is dedicated to God the Father, The Son, and The Holy Spirit...

My family, friends, pets and those that have gone before me...

I would like to thank Robert for his unconditional support, editing assistance, and extending his creative talents graciously for this assignment.

Contents

1. Divine Appointment...11

2. Peculiar People 23

3. Angels Watching Over Me.....................................29

4. Glorious Destiny..37

5. Perfect Vision..43

6. Sometimes In Your Life 51

7. Remember the Little Things.................................59

8. In the Beginning - "First Love"............................69

9. Picking Up the Pieces -"Broken Vessel" 73

10. The Perfect Union - "Faithful Friend" 81

11. Favor..87

12. This is My Father's World................................93

The Journey

One day I awoke and found myself on a journey called life

I really couldn't help but notice that there were

Bittersweet steps of ecstasy and strife…

As I crossed a bridge ahead, a fog was all I could see

Then suddenly a great fear arose deep inside of me…

I cried out, "Father Help me please", and fell down to my knees…

Just then I felt a gentle nudge that fashioned me to stand

And when I looked in front of me, He was holding out His hand…

Life is a journey that we must all take. What determines our destiny,

Are the choices that we make…

Come and discover exciting revelations of the Word of God,

Personal testimonies, songs, and rhymes…

Carefully written and presented in His time.

Let the Lord's Spirit speak to your heart

And receive His unfailing love that will never depart…

Chapter One

Divine Appointment

Chapter One:

Divine Appointment

"Hear oh Israel, the Lord is our God, the Lord alone. And you must love the Lord your God with all your heart, and all your soul, and your strength. And you must commit yourselves wholeheartedly to these commands I am giving you today. Repeat them again and again to your children. Talk about them when you are at home and when you are away on a journey, when you are lying down and when you were getting up again." *(Deuteronomy 6:4-7)*

Once upon a time, a real time, there was a little girl named "Baby Dor". This journey began many years ago through her eyes. That little girl was me. I cried out to God in my despair, and He heard me. Frightened and confused, I huddled amongst my draping clothes in the darkest place I could find in my closet. Yet almighty God in His sovereignty, reached for me.

My father called me "Baby Dor", He was a wise man with many talents. One particular gift he had was charisma. Whenever I was with him, I would observe his demeanor and really admired the way he would interact with people. He was also a generous man. I remember going with him to the grocery store when I was a little girl. At the check out counter there was an elderly woman in front of us. She didn't have enough money to pay for groceries she wanted to buy. My father, in his charming way, began a conversation with the cashier and before you knew it, he paid the balance on the woman's grocery bill. She began thanking my dad excessively; he just humbly accepted her appreciation and went on talking to the cashier as if it were business as usual.

My mom told me a story how she would listen to a children's program on the radio every Saturday morning. She heard this very talented young man singing a song called "Oh Johnny", and she thought, "Oh how I would like to meet him." Then one fateful day her friends set up a double date and lo and behold it was him, the man she listened to on the radio and dreamed to meet. That's right, my dad!

They married, had six children, and I'm one of them. After a while she found things were not as magical as she hoped they would be, because of a weakness she had discovered in him. The weakness was called alcoholism. I am not going to expound on the perils this disease caused in our home and how it devoured a very precious man's talents and dreams. But I am going to tell you that through this devastating time as a child, and being exposed to the demon of alcoholism, brought me to this incredible journey seeking out the true meaning of life.

One particular day when hiding in my closet, my "safe place" from the fury of the world around me, I cried out to God and shouted, "If you are real, then show me!" That moment, I felt an overwhelming and awesome presence. Was this really happening, or was I dreaming? Tears streamed down my face, mixed with the feelings of fear and joy all in one. With a quivering voice I asked, "Is that You God?" He replied "I am." Then I asked, "Will you show yourself to me?" And He answered, "I will." He made His presence known in a truly incredible way in my heart, it was unmistakable. From that moment forward, God has showed himself through many miraculous ways, changing and molding my steps through each incredible journey I have faced. That day is etched within my heart forever.

Through my journey, I have experienced many spiritual events. A few of these have been carefully selected for this book. I can think of an incident back in the late 1970's when I encountered a wonderful miracle while visiting the Immaculata retreat in Willmington,

Connecticut. Through the suggestion of a friend, I agreed to attend this retreat to intercede for my dad with the hope of one day seeing him free from alcoholism, so I could have the relationship that I had longed for. A lovely spirit-filled believer named Pat, who organized groups to attend these special events, was reunited with me after a long session of teaching, prayer, and worship. We decided to go to my room to share our experiences of the day. It was a day filled with praise and Honor to God. This left us feeling so high in the spirit that we did not want to come down from this mountain of worship with Him. It was approximately 3:00am and we both realized we needed to get some sleep to be ready for the last day of our retreat. We were standing in the center of a very small room. As we embraced each other to say "goodnight", we both experienced burning warmth in our hearts. Before I could say another word, I saw the most incredible blinding white light surrounding us. I was able to catch a glimpse of a transparent arm and the pure white sleeve of a garment. We both had experienced a "Divine Appointment." Neither of us has ever forgotten that treasured visitation!

Unfortunately, my dad had experienced the repercussions of the reckless living conditions he had placed on his body. He suffered diabetes since childhood. And due to his diabetic condition, and not caring for his body, he was left a double amputee. By not being able to get around like he was used to, he was forced to give up the alcohol. Being the aggressive man he was, he could not bear the life he was now faced with. Shortly after losing his legs, he tried to commit suicide but fortunately he didn't succeed. My family and I continued to pray for him. Even though there was a lot of confusion in our home when growing up, one thing stood strong, the relationship that we had with one another. We were all very close. Even though my dad was battling this disease, he remained a very loving man. Along with my mom, the peacemaker, they instilled in us the strong bond of love and respect we have for each other. My brothers were older and always looked out for me and my two sisters.

I always have fond memories of how we all stuck together like glue. When I was around seven years old, I stepped on a large nail, which punctured deep into my little foot. I hobbled toward the house screaming and crying. My oldest brother Larry heard me and ran outside. Without any delay he grabbed me, and compassionately carried me down the street several blocks to the doctor's office. Along with his compassionate heart, he is also a talented drummer. He would practice playing the drums on anything he could, sometimes even me! The next in line is my middle brother Bill. He brought to us a strong sense of faith and reverence toward God, always reading the Bible. Even today he carries the passion to serve as a pillar of strength, and always with a smile. I remember his 12th birthday party. My mom made one of her wonderful cakes and invited some of his friends over. I was so excited to come to his birthday party since it was in our home. I thought I would dress really special for this occasion. When my brother Bill took one look at me in my white tee shirt and nurse's hat, the expression on his face was priceless. You see, Bill was conventional and I was just too eccentric. Needless to say, we were very different from each other. But as years went on, we both learned to understand our unique personalities. Then there is my youngest brother Marc, the charismatic one, with an edifying personality. All my brothers were exceptional football players, especially Marc. I was known as the "sister of Marc" in school, because he was the star football player. I can recall talking in class without permission one day and was sent to the corner of the room (I wonder how that would fly today), and my brother Marc was a room messenger that came to my classroom. I remember feeling horrified when I saw my brother coming through the door. My teacher gave him a generous welcome and then he looked toward the back of the room and spotted me in the corner. He told my teacher that I was his sister and asked her what I had done. As I bowed my head in embarrassment, I heard Marc talking to my teacher and the next thing I knew I was back in my seat and she was pleased to hear that he was my brother. Wow, I thought, I just gained favor being Marc's sister. He was always popular but never haughty; he had a humble spirit then, and carries this same attribute today.

Along with my three brothers, I had two sisters. Mary is my older sister. She was the feisty one, and still is today. Although loving and kind, if she knew someone hurt you, watch out! If you wanted a strong fighter on your team, she was the girl. I can remember her bringing home our first dog. Even though our parents did not like this idea, she fought the case and won! She still has a heart for these precious creations of God today. Our baby of the family is Lisa. She is the corporate girl, organized, and structured with a generous and gentle spirit added to the mix. What stands out most in my memory when we were young, is the quiet conversation we shared. We would lay next to each other on the bed with our legs folded and crossed, just enjoying each other's company without many words at all. Sometimes we just did a lot of giggling. But one thing is for sure; all my brothers and sisters are beautiful, unique and precious. Most of all we share a common bond - we all love the Lord!

When my dad was hospitalized after trying to end his life, one night he was calling out "Baby Dor" several times. The doctor asked my mom if she understood why he would call out these words. She said

"That's the name he called one of my daughters." I had visited him days before with my bible in hand, reading him God's Holy Word. But all he would do is look straight through me and hit the bar above his head with his hand. When my mom told me what the doctor had said, I came to visit him the next day. He lifted himself up with the bar above his head and said to me "Baby Dor, I don't know what I have done to you, but all I know is that the devil wants my soul." I said, "No daddy, he can't have it!" He then asked me to forgive him, and I said "I already have, but more importantly, you need to ask for God to forgive you and ask His precious Son Jesus Christ into your heart and receive His gift of Salvation!" He did, and I wept with him.

From that moment on, I was able to begin the relationship with my dad that I had dreamt about. Through the short time he remained here on earth I was able to discover even more of the many beautiful facets of who he really was. He was not only a loving, kind man with a generous heart, but he also had a prophetic gift. Unfortunately, he was only able to exercise it for a short time. As it is written in Hosea 4:9 "We perish for lack of knowledge."

Some years later, my father was once again in the hospital. His heart was failing quickly. He had become lethargic and weak. I called his room and my mom answered the phone, I told her I had prepared his favorite meal, homemade raviolis made from scratch, which he had taught me to make. One more talent my father was known for was his awesome cooking. I often watched him and paid attention when he cooked, so one day I too could carry on this talent. Then my mother said "Why don't you tell your father yourself?" and as I started to tell him, I heard him say in a faint, yet piercing voice "Baby Dor, I love you" and just then, I heard my mom scream and the phone was disconnected.

I left immediately for the hospital. As I began to leave my driveway and head down the street, I heard the Lord speak to me. When you know His voice, it is very clear when He is speaking to you, in whatever manner it comes. Just as it is written in John 10:26: "My sheep hear my voice, and I know them, and they follow me." Then I heard the Lord speak to my heart, "I took your daddy home." Since the time of meeting God in my closet, I have always revered Him. But at this moment, I felt like a spoiled little girl that just didn't get her way. I cried out "NO" you just can't take him away, this is too soon! And the Lord replied, "Go now, your mother is waiting for you" and I replied, "I can't move" and then began travailing in my spirit - crying from the depths of my soul. Just then, I felt as if there was a ball of extreme warmth swirling from the top of my head down to my toes. I began to feel a peace that was so wonderful. I had experienced the "peace that surpasses all understanding" as it is written in Philippians 4:7. Composing myself, I headed to the hospital where my mom was waiting to tell me the news. With the peace that God had given me, I was able to be a comfort to her.

We enter this world upon divine appointment. The events that take place are strategically formed and fashioned for each of us to embrace. What we choose to do during our time here on earth will greatly affect the implications of life as we live it. Our choices not only affect our lives but those around us!

Chapter Two

———⟨⟩———

Peculiar People

Chapter Two:

Peculiar People

"But ye are a chosen generation, a royal priesthood, a holy nation, a peculiar people; that ye should show forth the praise of Him who hath called you out of darkness into His marvelous light."

(1 Peter 2:9)

Years ago, when I attended college, there was a very special young man I met waiting outside the student center. This young man was patiently waiting by the door in his motorized wheelchair. When I approached him, I asked him if he'd like to enter the student center. He quietly responded "yes", so I open the door and let us both in. I asked if I could sit with him and he responded with a blushingly sweet smile. I knew this would be the beginning of a treasured friendship. His name was Wally. I admired his courage for attending college by himself having muscular dystrophy; especially in the 1970's when facilities were not as handicapped-accessible as they are today. I asked him how long he had waited at the door and he answered, "For some time." I was saddened by this answer and thought to myself, "How can people just walk by and not notice him at the door?" His hair was long, especially his bangs that would cover his eyes. He could not lift his hands or arms up high enough due to his limited movement; although he did have enough mobility to control his motorized wheelchair. When he would try to push his head back to move his bangs, his head would just get locked back and he'd have to struggle to regain the upright position.

One day, I offered to come over to his home and cut his hair. He graciously accepted. When I arrived, his parents were gracious and thankful for my help. I wanted to make this simple necessity of life a magical adventure, so that Wally would feel comfortable. When I finished, sitting before me was a beautiful young man with the fire of life in his eyes that were now revealed for all to see. I asked him if he had ever danced, he said "no" blushingly. So I took his delicate hand in mine and danced with Wally as if we were in a ballroom filled with sparkling lights and the sweetest music ever heard. Wally and I began to laugh so hard that we could hardly breathe. When I left, I began to cry tears of joy on my drive home. Fellowshipping with one of God's humble children gave me a feeling of happiness.

The day had come when I was called to move away, so Wally and I agreed to write to each other because email was unheard of at that time. My journey had taken me to another chapter of life that was filled with many new surprises ahead. I had sent Wally my first letter, but he did not respond. I felt sure something had happened. Then, just as I'd imagined, I received a letter from his mom telling me Wally had passed away from pneumonia. She wanted to thank me for the joy I had brought to her son in this life. My response was; "It was Wally who taught me so much and gave me so much joy." He inspired me to look through the eyes of each person and take a glimpse of what's inside. You may find the hidden treasure of friendship, love and unforgettable memories; even if it is for only a short season of time.

Sometimes people come into your life for a season and the "love print" they leave lasts a lifetime. Even if the only reason is to leave you with one precious memory, something to be cherished, learned, or a piece of history to carry with you on your journey. I have many of these treasured friends - you know who you are!

Chapter Three

Angels Watching Over Me

Chapter Three:
Angels Watching Over Me

"Cornelius (Roman army officer) was a devout man who feared the God of Israel, as did his entire household. He gave generously to charity and was a man who regularly prayed to God. One afternoon about 3:00, he had a vision in which he saw an Angel of God coming toward him. "Cornelius" the Angel said. Cornelius stared at him in terror. "What is it sir" he asked the Angel. And the Angel replied. "Your prayers and gifts to the poor have not gone unnoticed by God!" *(Acts 10: 2-4)*

I have a beautiful niece Alicia, she is one of God's precious treasures from heaven. She truly knows what it's like to live every day only imaging being able to do some of the simple daily tasks in life most of us just take for granted. She was born with muscular atrophy. Therefore, her only form of mobility is through her motorized wheelchair.

I recently had the privilege to participate in one of the Annual Jerry Lewis Muscular Dystrophy "Lock up" Fund Raisers. I called Alecia to help me put together a short video ad I was working on; to help raise funds for this worthy cause. She graciously agreed. Even though the miles between us are many, she is always near to my heart. In compiling the information, a greater awareness arose in me of how life would be in her journey, as well for others which shared a similar physical handicap. Her awesome ability to smile through the pain she experiences every day is such a monumental feat, that most people cannot even comprehend. Her beautiful heart is filled with love, compassion, mercy, and the desire to do the fruitful works of God with her delicate hands. She completely embraces the call of God in her life here on earth. Her journey is one that is honored and admired not only by me, but those who are blessed to be a part of her life.

I can recall one visit when my brother Bill, his wife Laura, and Alecia came to see us in Florida one summer. We all went to Universal studios in Orlando on a typical hot and humid summer day. I can only imagine how uncomfortable Alecia was in her motorized wheelchair and body brace. She smiled often and endured the surroundings of a hectic day at the theme park. People were all around us, pushing and shoving to be the first ones to enter an attraction. I watched as people would stare, and to my amazement, even act rude, without compassion toward my niece. She didn't seem to notice; she just smiled and enjoyed the journey that she had encountered for the day. I thought to myself, "How dare they treat this special treasure from God in this way!?" But then, I also noticed there were other people that showed compassion and kindness toward her. I realized how much our own actions can make a difference, and turn the darkness into light.

When it comes to angel intervention, there have been many instances I can recall in my life, but just a couple events I will share.

When I was about ten years old, we lived in a raised ranch style home with four bedrooms, and a large bedroom in a finished cellar where my brothers had their room. I remember my brothers were gone and I went to go sleep in their room. Soon after, I had a strange feeling over me and was compelled to go sleep in my own room upstairs. Since the night before, I had dreamt of a fire burning in a home that I didn't recognize. During the night, I was awakened by a nudge and heard someone calling my name. When I awoke, all I could see was smoke filling the room. I immediately ran to the bathroom down the hall and grabbed some washcloths, ran them under water and went to wake up my mom. The Lord had inspired me to take this action since I would not have known what to do on my own. She was coughing, and when I put the cloth over her face she woke up and we both went into the room where my dad was sleeping. You couldn't see anything. The bed was in flames and the room thick with smoke. My dad had fallen asleep with a lit cigarette. He was a heavy man, but my mom and I rolled him off the bed onto the floor and I quickly took the flaming king size mattress down the hall, out the kitchen door, and threw it over the deck railing while my mom called the fire department. When they arrived, they could not believe that a very petite, ten year old girl could carry a heavy mattress that distance while it was in flames, and lift it up over the deck railing to fall seven feet to the ground. They said that I saved my family. But I know it was the Lord, through angel intervention, that saved our lives that day!

In another incident, a friend invited me to a prayer meeting some years ago. As people were entering the building, I could hear some chatter amongst them. They were saying with amazement "Look, there's that bum that just walked in." I did not pay any attention to this and sat down. When the meeting started, we all joined hands and closed our eyes for prayer. I reached out to hold the hand of my friend on one side, and then out to the person on the other side. I did not take notice of who was next to me. I just closed my eyes and began to pray. Suddenly, I felt incredible warmth coming from the stranger's hand. Involuntarily, I lifted the stranger's hand and kissed it. As I did, I opened my eyes and to my amazement it was him, the stranger people were chatting about. After prayer, he seemed to just disappear. I wanted to find him to talk with him, but he was gone and no one saw him leave. A woman came up to me after the meeting and said she was sitting across the room from me. She said during the prayer, she had her eyes open and saw a beautiful white light around me. She wanted to shout it out for all to see, but she couldn't speak a word until after the prayer meeting was finished. I knew I had a "close encounter" of the Angelic kind!

"Don't be afraid to show hospitality to strangers for some who have done this have entertained Angels without realizing it!" (Hebrews 13:2)

Chapter Four

Glorious Destiny

Chapter Four:

Glorious Destiny

"You will keep on guiding me with your counsel, leading me to glorious destiny." *(Psalm 73:24)*

———————— ⁓⬡⬡⬡⬡⁓ ————————

We must embrace the call upon our lives and discover the true riches that are waiting to be revealed. Through God's Holy Spirit, faith, obedience, and studying His Holy Word, we find the answer to life's most pressing question: "What is my purpose here?"

In the Book of Esther, you will find an account of a Jewish orphan who became Queen of Persia. Through a crucial act of obedience, she saved her people from total destruction. This story is told and even celebrated today as the "Feast of Purim." This holiday commemorates the deliverance of the Jewish Nation brought about by God's divine power through Esther. "If I have found favor with the king, and if it pleases the king to grant my request, I ask that my life and the lives of my people will be spared. For my people and I have been sold to those who would kill, slaughter, and annihilate us. If we had merely been sold as slaves, I could remain quiet, for that would be too trivial a matter to warrant disturbing the king." (Esther 7:3-4)

It's a fascinating journey of a noble Jewish orphan that becomes queen through her heroic effort in remaining faithful, humble and obedient to God; even though it meant risking her life to save others. In the Book of Esther, we learn how God actually has His hand in the situations we face; rather than certain events being mere coincidences. We also discover that God's plans will not be moved by evil actions of men. Our Father often uses signs to communicate with us through His Holy Spirit. By being aware of these signs, we can partake in God's blessings not only for ourselves, but for others as well. For example, the favor that was bestowed upon Esther is what saved her people. Had she ignored the signs that were given to her, God would have found someone else that would have listened and taken action. We can obtain God's favor by seeking His will, walking in His ways, and being filled with His Holy Spirit. Be sure to explore Esther's fascinating journey of courage and faith by reading the Book of Esther in the Old Testament.

Often there are times when we feel clouded and confused, and the call of our destiny seems distant. Sometimes, we can't imagine that God in His infinite Glory could call us for such a great mission.

Well, He can and He does! There is no insignificant person called by God, he chooses us according to His purpose. We are each called in our own unique way, using the talents with which we are gifted.

When I was preparing for this book, I encountered many distractions. I have an outgoing personality and a desire to be around family and friends almost all of my waking hours. I had to discipline myself and organize my time with God, family, and friends. Then, after the necessary appointments of each day, I had to find quiet time to write. What a feat! One particular day when feeling the opposition from around my circle of life, I let discouragement befall me. I was overwhelmed by all of the nagging daily tasks that were trying to steal the joy of my journey. I set out to walk my dog, a Siberian husky. Just as we reached the familiar corner of our usual path, I began to weep uncontrollably. My dog stopped, looked back at me as if to say, "What's wrong with you, it's a beautiful day in the neighborhood!" just then, I looked up through my teary eyes, and saw all around me beautiful hearts. I am not sure of the name, but they grow in Florida and the green leaves of this wild plant are shaped exactly like hearts. I began to laugh and cry at the same time. Now my husky looked back at me with a look that only a dog owner could know. His look was one of, "I told you so!" To me, this was a reminder that even when we don't feel it, God is there, and His love never leaves us. I then said to God, "Thank you for this awesome reminder of your love, but what would really make me happy today is if I saw you write in the clouds, I love you." I can't even believe I would ask God such a thing! But to my amazement, as my husky and I walked further on, I heard the Lord say, "Look up" and as I did, up in the clouds I could see a formation. I saw an arm and hand with the thumb, pointer and pinky fingers up as to form the sign language hand signal of "I love you." I dropped to my knees by the side of the road and cried out to God, thanking Him for hearing my prayer, and answering me even though I did not expect an answer to that request. Did you ever ask God for something that you did not really expect Him answer? Well, I did that glorious day, and He answered me.

Love the Lord your God with all your heart and He will bring you to your glorious destiny!

Chapter Five

Perfect Vision

Chapter Five:

Perfect Vision

"He speaks in dreams, in visions of the night when deep sleep falls on people as they lie in bed." *(Job 33:15)*

God's Holy Spirit can speak to us in many ways: by dreams, visions, silent whispers, and signs and wonders. Sometimes when God is speaking people don't hear Him. We need to learn how to recognize His voice, as there is no confusion with God. He will always confirm and clearly state His message. The more consecrated we become; the greater the Holy Spirit will manifest in our lives. As we walk with Christ, and strive to walk in His excellence, our vision becomes clearer. Deceitful and compromising deeds become evident through the discernment of the Holy Spirit.

The following story was given to me through the inspiration of the Holy Spirit. There was a little girl named Leah. Every day she would walk to school by the same path. One rainy day, she met a stranger along the way. He seemed harmless, safe and strong. He asked Leah if she would like a lift to school. She thought that would be a good idea, since she was wearing her new shoes her mom had just bought for her. Her mom worked so hard to get them, and Leah wore them proudly! She accepted the stranger's proposition for the lift since he seemed so strong and kind. As he lifted Leah up with his seemingly strong arms, a sense of familiarity arose from deep within her. You see, Leah's dad had gone home to be with the Lord a couple of years ago, leaving behind Leah and her mom. She only knew her dad for a short time during her seven years of life.

Leah was trusting and innocent. She said to the man, "My name is Leah, what is yours?" The man replied, "My name is Deceiver." Leah replied, "Hum, what a strange name for such a strong, gentle and kind man such as you." Deceiver just smiled and walked on. As they continued to walk further on, the rain began to pour down upon them. Suddenly, Deceiver stumbled into a large puddle of water. He couldn't see that beneath the water was a pot hole large enough to catch his left foot securely. He tried to shake his foot fervently to free himself, but could not. Deceiver hastily put Leah on the ground and angrily told her to go the rest of the way alone. Leah offered to help, but Deceiver just became more agitated and shouted "Just leave me alone!" So Leah turned and began running with her eyes closed as fast and she could. When she opened her eyes, she could see her principal in the distance waiting for her with the doors of the school opened wide.

When she reached the principal waiting at the door, huffing and puffing she said, "I met the most amazing man on my way to school today." Her principal replied, "How so?" "Well", said Leah, "His name was Deceiver and he carried me part of the way to school this morning." The principal asked, "And why was he so amazing?" "Well", said Leah, "At first when it started to rain and I saw him, he looked so strong, fearless, and kind. But as we began to go on, he walked into a large puddle and got his foot stuck. When he put me down and I looked back at him, he didn't look very strong, fearless or kind anymore. His face was dark and cold. His body looked sick and frail. And his voice was mean and frightful! So I prayed "Father help me!" as I ran with my eyes closed. And when I opened them, there you were with the doors opened wide waiting for me."

Sometimes, we can be too trusting in people and situations that seem harmless, especially when they seem to have God's signature. Matthew 18:2-4 states, "I tell you the truth, unless you change and become like little children, you will never enter the kingdom of heaven." So we must have child-like faith to enter the kingdom, a faith that is simple, pure, and unclouded. But, it is just as important to have discernment of the Holy Spirit with maturity, which will protect us from the deceptions of the enemy. We know we can trust our Father in heaven completely, without any reserve, and practice that pure, child-like faith. We cannot take that same trust and immediately hand it over to someone else without any further thought; this is where the gift of discernment comes in. This advice may seem like common sense, but there are those who take it too far and shut out most of the people around them. In the end, we just have to allow the Holy Spirit to reveal the truth to us.

It is much too easy to get led astray by deceitful words and compromising deeds. We've all been deceived by the adversary a time or two in this way. The most important thing to remember is that when it becomes apparent you fell for the bait the adversary placed in your path, repent wholeheartedly before the Lord and let His forgiveness cleanse and restore you. So the next time the enemy attacks, you will be prepared and you won't be so easily beguiled.

Another deception from the adversary is the disguise he uses to steal away blessings of healing. One example of this is when I was healed by the Lord of migraine headaches, which I had suffered since childhood. My daughter was a newborn baby and I was lying down next to her on the bed for a nap. All of the sudden a blinding white spot would appear just before feeling the pain and nausea of a migraine. I immediately panicked. I thought, "How am I going to care for her if she wakes up?" The pain would be so bad I had to keep the room dark and stay very still until it would pass. Sometimes the migraine would last for several hours. If you've experienced a severe migraine, you know the pain can be debilitating. I began to cry out "Lord please help me so I can care for my daughter." Instantly I felt the Holy Spirit cover me with warmth. The blinding spot diminished, my headache disappeared, and the sickly feeling was completely gone! I began praising His Holy Name! I shared this miraculous healing with those around me and gave God the glory.

A couple years later, I started to see the same migraine blind spot forming. Fear rose up in me, and I thought, "Is my healing gone?" Then I said out loud, "NO, I am healed in Jesus' name!" and immediately the spot disappeared. I realized this was a counterfeit from the deceiver, which is Satan. After that I thought, "The devil isn't going to try that with me again now that I am privy to his deception." Wrong! The deceiver is relentless. Sure enough he had tried again, but I stood my ground on the solid rock, which is Christ Jesus. I am thankful for this victory, and that I have spiritual eyes to see the truth; for His truth sets us free!

Knowledge in fighting spiritual battles will help us gain victory and freedom over the wiles of the enemy. As my son always reminds me, "One of the greatest lies the devil has, is trying to make us believe that he doesn't exist." Beware; the deceiver tries to distract us from our communion with God. For it is our communion with God that empowers us to stay in His will and accomplish great things for Him!

Be sure to put on the full armor of God every day when you awake. Prepare for the battle, worship in spirit and truth. Intercede for your loved ones and country, and study God's Holy Word. "Stand your ground, putting on the belt of truth and the body armor of God's righteousness." (Ephesians 6:14)

Chapter Six

Sometimes In Your Life

Chapter Six:

Sometimes In Your Life

"Love means doing what God has commanded us, and He has commanded us to love one another just as you heard from the beginning." *(2 John 1:6)*

Try taking one day out your life without anyone around you. No family, no friends, and no pets. Not even the cell phone, computer, or any type of entertainment. It may feel great at first, "ahh", you may say, "peace and quiet." But after a while, you will miss them. You've heard the expression, "No man is an island."

I met a very special man one day in a church I was attending some years ago. His name was George. He had a childlike nature due to an emotional and somewhat physical handicap. I had observed the way the children of the church loved to gather around him. He walked slowly with a cane, but one thing I will never forget; he always wore a smile on his face!

George lived alone, and did not have any family near him, so I would invite him to come over on certain holidays, and quite often visit him at his home. He loved to go out to dine at this one particular Chinese restaurant. So we would make it a habit every so often to go there and celebrate a meal together. I watched him journey through his uncomplicated world. One thing was certain, he loved the Lord! This was evident to anyone that would look upon his humble stature and sparkling eyes. Some years had passed and George's health began to fail. He could no longer care for himself, so he was placed in a nursing home. I received a phone call from the nursing home one day and they told me that George was failing fast. He was struggling with pain and hanging onto life by a thread. I came to visit him and saw this once beautiful, loving, and kind man that I had fellowshipped with. Now he was distressed and curled up in the fetal position. He was frightened and afraid to let go of this world. I asked George if he trusted me. He shook his head as to motion yes, struggling to look up at me. I said to him, "The angels are waiting to carry you home to heaven." You see, George's mind was like a child and someone told him that he was going to die. This frightened him, and the fear of death became a big, scary monster to George. I simply told him the truth, and the truth comforted him. I kissed his forehead and said, "Goodbye for now, my friend, I'll see you on the other side." He managed to struggle out a little smile and closed his eyes. The next day the nursing home called me and said "George went home." This is the poem I wrote in his honor:

Suffer the little children to come unto me
And forbid them not
For of such is the kingdom of heaven (Matt 19:14)

The children gathered around you
Because they knew your child-like faith

The children gathered around you
Because they knew your unconditional love

The children gathered around you
Because they knew you were sent from heaven above

Your smiling eyes and gentle stare
That let us know, you always care

No matter what, no matter how, no matter why

Your love was always pure and free
And always seemed just for me

Oh how I was blessed to share such love and precious times
Even laughter and some tears
And still stayed close throughout the years

As time when on, we kept that bond
But it hurt me so, as I felt your fear

But how could you know, there is peace waiting there
Because you hung on so dear
To memories that just wanted to keep you here

Your painful smile, now piercing right through me
It was now clear, what has to be

When I kissed your smiling face my friend
I knew your journey here had come to an end
So I quietly sighed, "My love for you will always abide"
And whispered, "I'll see you on the other side."

Sometimes the passing through this world to the next is a peaceful journey. I had the privilege of knowing for a short time a dear lady that I called friend. She was called home to heaven in her eighties in a very peaceful way. She just fell asleep in her favorite chair and awoke on the other side. I wrote this poem in her honor:

Sometimes in your life
Someone comes along and makes your heart smile
Just like a sweet love song

A friend who sparkles with sunlight...even in the rain
Who cares for you, even through the pain

Eyes filled with compassion for every one she knew
And ears that listened tenderly, to the deepest hurt in you

A heart so true and pure
I will always know one thing for sure...
That even though, she made me feel like a shining star...
That is what, Faye, I know you are...

I am reminded of the precious words that were spoken through my daughter-in-law Janet's grandmother before she went home to be with the Lord. This dear woman was in her 91st year of life. Her mind was sharp but her body was breaking down. I remember talking to my daughter-in-law's mother on the telephone as she was telling me that her mother was hanging on to life by a thread. When she told her mother to let go and let the angels carry her to heaven so that she can be with the Lord and her husband, she replied, "Heaven is way too big, I'll never find him!" Sometimes we too look at a situation and see it bigger than it really is.

May we always find comfort in knowing that when our journey here ends, a new one unfolds as we pass though to the other side.

Chapter Seven

Remember the Little Things

Chapter Seven:

Remember the Little Things

"He who is faithful in a very little (thing) is faithful also in much, and he who is dishonest and unjust in a very little thing is dishonest and unjust also in much." *(Luke 16:10)*

This was a favorite saying around our home, "Do well in the little things and God will bless you with bigger things." With the bigger things, come bigger responsibilities.

When my son Davin was seven years old I can recall driving home from an event that left me with an unusual headache, not too severe, but just enough to be annoying. I started to rub my head to relieve the tension and just then, I felt these two gentle hands reach up to my head from the back of me. My son began to pray for me. I was moved to tears that this gentle-spirited boy would reach out to me in this way. My headache disappeared and I knew that God has a special plan for this gifted and treasured child.

Having an anointed call on our life also comes with great opposition from the adversary. One the most frightening times I can recall was when my son was nine years old. We were all at my mom's home getting ready to attend the funeral service for my dad. The house was filled with family and friends preparing to leave together. My mom had a small toy poodle named LeeLee that would get very anxious around a lot commotion. So as people were leaving the house to get into their cars, LeeLee escaped. My mind was so clouded and with all the confusion going on, I did not notice that the dog was missing. We all got into our cars and headed to the funeral home. When we arrived, I saw that my daughter was there but not my son. I panicked and frantically asked, "Who brought Davin?" Then I realized he was not with any of us. I felt devastated that he was left back at the house. Just as we were about to go back to get him, a phone call came to the funeral home letting us know that my cousin, Betty Ann, had come to the house, because she wasn't sure where the funeral home was. She found Davin there sitting in the breezeway with LeeLee. When I questioned him as to why he did not get into one of the cars, he answered, "I had to get LeeLee", and then I said "Were you frightened when we all left?" and he replied, "No, I prayed to God and he spoke in my heart that someone would come and get me."

When Davin was ten years old, we discovered he had a talent for baseball. His first year in this sport revealed he had this natural talent for the game. He was gifted the ability of powerful hitting, along with great fielding and pitching. Having this talent, the motivational drive, and love for the game, you would think things would go pretty smooth for this young man. But this wasn't the case; he encountered many struggles along this journey. Even from places that I would not have imagined. There were unprovoked attacks that came from some teammates, and even coaches and umpires. But through these life trials, my son's integrity was being tried and tested.

One hot summer day at a little league baseball game, I remember Davin getting up to bat and I can recall the spectators yelling at my son "Get a homerun, or let's go home!" repeatedly. I thought, "Why are they depending on my son to win the game when this is a team sport?" Sure enough, my son was listening to the crowd and at the first pitch thrown, he swung for the fence. The umpire shouted, "Strike one!" My excited shouts began to quiet with warranted concerns. The more they shouted, the more pressure was put on my son. I could see the joy of the game was hidden by the now eager shouts of the crowd. The next pitch, the ball went foul way over the fence. So now, expectations were really high, especially since the outcome of the game was riding on my son's shoulders.

Finally, the last pitch of the game, and from my perspective and the spectators on our side, the pitch of the ball was too low to swing. So my son just watched it go by. The umpire yelled, "Strike!" and that was the last out of the game. My son threw the bat down and mumbled under his breath his disapproval of the umpires' call. Although I disagreed as well, my son should not have acted in this way. I ran after him, since the game was over and we obviously did not win. He was a young teen at this time and was still building character. I said to him, "Remember the little things, God is watching to see our reactions even when we are treated unfairly."

My son dropped to his knees by the fence and I heard him ask God to forgive him for his bad attitude. I stood back in admiration as this young man humbled himself before God, not even concerned that his peers may be watching. Then I witnessed him walk over to the umpire to apologize for his poor choice of actions. As I made my way back to the car, the umpire stopped me and said, "I had never encountered such integrity in such a talented young man." I knew there would be many rocky roads ahead, but one thing I was sure of, my son knew the meaning of "Remember the little things!" Integrity is what makes us really shine even in the most difficult situations.

We don't wrestle with the love we have for each other, remember there is a battle at war trying to cause dissention amongst us. We are not perfect, and sometimes we don't always make the right choices initially. But when we can humble ourselves and realize what is at work against us, we then can combat this deceptive plot to destroy the true love we have for each other instilled in us by God's design.

As it is written in Ephesians 6:12, "For we wrestle not against flesh and blood, but against principalities, against powers, against the rulers of the darkness of this world, against spiritual wickedness in high places."

Do you know someone special in your life that just doesn't seem to want to get along? Love them, encourage them, and never cease to pray for them!

I wrote this song for my son Davin:

Remember the Little Things

Wonder what the Lord will have for you today
My blue-eyed boy,
For life seems to slip away

Looking in your innocent eyes
I see your child-like dreams
The vision of the Master's plan
To do the little things with humble hands

(chorus)
Struggles that never end it seems,
The laughter and joy that promise brings,
The tears that heal the wounded soul
How sweet the sound when you reach your goal
To hear Him say, "Well done, my son"
Remember the little things....

Baseball bats and fishing poles,
Treasure hunts, and GI Joes
There'll be hurts and pains in the fields you sow
Which will bring you strength as you grow
Through...

(chorus)

Struggles that never end it seems,
The laughter and joy that promise brings,
The tears that heal the wounded soul
How sweet the sound when you reach your goal
To hear Him say, "Well done, my son"
Remember the little things....

And when you get to the place of your dreams,
Don't forget my son... remember the little things...

Chapter Eight

―――⚬⚬⚬⚬―――

In the Beginning

"First Love"

Chapter 8:

In the Beginning - "First Love"

"I am the Alpha and Omega, the beginning and the end", says the Lord God, "I am the one who is, who always was, and who is still to come, the Almighty One." *(Rev. 1:8)*

"Nevertheless I have somewhat against thee, because thou hast left thy first love." *(Rev. 2:4)*

God is calling us to come back to our first love. Remember the day when you first met that special someone you couldn't wait to be with? You would talk for hours. Groom yourself tastefully and adorn yourself with your best attire. You would give freely of yourself to the needs of that special someone. You'd take the time to truly get to know each other; with encouraging praise and careful criticism. As the relationship progresses, it takes on different and new challenges. Sometimes instead of growing into a deeper, peaceful, and secure love; jealousy, unforgiveness, and strife enters the relationship. The passionate fire once bright becomes dimmed by the enticing persuasions of the world. Communication decreases and complacency creeps in, setting the stage for failure.

Our relationship with God, if not carefully kept in check, can fall into a similar situation. When we first receive this precious gift of salvation that comes to us through the Cross at Calvary, we are born again, becoming a new creation in Christ. Where all the old nature is put to death and the new creation emerges. We receive God's Holy Spirit, which is His working power in the earth. Initially, we feel the awesome fire burning bright within our soul along with unspeakable joy. Out of every breath we took, flowed living words of glory to God for His greatness. Then the struggles of life set in. Financial difficulties, bitterness, envy, and strife causing many distractions that would keep us far from that pure joy we had once experienced. Oh, the belief in Him would still be present, and the reverence tucked away for a rainy day, but the passionate fire of the first love would now be reduced to a flicker.

Ignite that holy fire and give the first fruits of your love and dedication to God. Praise and worship Him with pure love. You will experience a wonderful relationship with God and those around you as well! You see, a strong relationship with God is the primary foundation for the relationships you form with others.

Chapter Nine

———⚬———

Picking Up the Pieces

"Broken Vessel"

Chapter Nine:

Picking Up the Pieces - "Broken Vessel"

"The Lord is close to the brokenhearted, He rescues those who are crushed in spirit." *(Psalm 34:18)*

"And He shall rule them with a scepter of iron, as when earthen pots are broken in pieces and His power over them shall be like that which I myself have received from my father." *(Rev.2:27)*

In the process of preparing for this book, the Lord sent me out on a journey. He placed in my heart the desire to go to The Holy Land Experience in Orlando, Florida. Before I headed out on this journey, there were two words playing over and over in my mind. They were "broken vessel." I wrote these words down in my journal and then went on my way. The Lord also spoke to me that I would meet someone there with a message for me. When I arrived at The Holy Land Experience, I immediately looked around for any potential person that would have the message the Lord spoke of. In doing so, I met many lovely people who worked there with a true heart for God. I prayed and fellowshipped with them, and found that they truly lived the scripture written in Col. 3:23 "And whatsoever ye do, do it heartily, as to the Lord, and not unto men."

At the end of a most enjoyable and blessed day, I had completely forgotten about looking for someone with the message. I was about to leave the park, when in the corner of my eye, a woman by a large rock caught my attention. Her head was down and it appeared she was deep in prayer. I went over to her and stood by her until she would lift her head so I could offer to pray with her. She felt my presence and immediately looked up at me. She said, "It's you!" I replied, "Excuse me?" She explained that when she saw me earlier in the day, the Lord spoke to her to give me a message. When she tried to approach me it seemed as if I had disappeared. Then she said to me, "I keep hearing the words 'broken vessel', does this mean anything to you?" I exclaimed, "Yes, these are the words the Lord gave me as I left my home to come here!" She told me her name was Liz and she had a graceful and elegant spirit. We hugged, cried and prayed together as we both witnessed the beauty of God's grace.

She told me of a vision that she had of a broken vessel being carefully put back together by the Master's Hand. As she elaborated on the vision, I could see that I was that "broken vessel" carefully put back together piece by piece to form a new creation for His Glory!

Liz, reminding me of the beautiful butterfly, elegant and free spirited, made me think of the butterfly's journey. I once heard a story of a young boy trying to help a butterfly as it struggled to leave its cocoon. The boy's intention was innocent, but the act of his intervention left the butterfly helpless, defenseless, and never able to fly. This isn't what God intended for this beautiful and colorful creation of His. You see, God designed every facet of the butterfly's journey. When he is a caterpillar, he sheds his final outer skin which becomes the cocoon to protect the remarkable transformation that takes place inside. Then, in just the right moment, the butterfly begins to emerge by piercing a small hole in the cocoon and the struggle begins. During this struggle, fluid is being forced into the wings so the butterfly will be able to fly free from its cocoon. Due to the boy's attempt to expedite this process, the butterfly could not fully develop and therefore could not be all it was intended to be.

It is difficult when we see someone that we love who is struggling. We too, like that boy, want to step in and ease the pain. As I learned with my beautiful daughter Deneana you can't always "rescue and release." By this I mean we just can't jump in and save the day, without allowing the lessons God intended for us to be experienced. We can assist and be a blessing by example through divine coaching.

"Train up a child in the way he should go: and when he is old, he will not depart from it." (Proverbs 22:6) I wrote this poem for my daughter:

Daughter

Daughter, precious parcel from above
God has formed you with His love
You were gently placed within our care,
To nurture and guide you while you're here
Even through your darkest fear,
When things around you seem so unclear
You can call upon Jesus' Holy name
And things will never be the same
For the Lord will shine His light so bright
That even the stars won't know it is night
And give you strength to make it through your days
For great and wondrous are His ways

When my daughter decided to leave college and start a family, I was disheartened. I thought it would be best for her to finish school then start her family. The key word here is "I." So she went her way and lo and behold my first grandchild was on the way! When my first grandchild was born, I remember being in the delivery room with my daughter to assist with the blessed event. All I remember is when this beautiful baby boy entered into this world I yelled joyously, "I have a boy!" The doctor laughed so hard he could barely finish the delivery. My daughter, well, she just sighed "Oh mom!" and there before us was a beautiful baby boy! She went on to bring two more precious parcels into the family. When my granddaughters were born, I was warned by my daughter at each delivery, "And mom, don't yell, I have a girl!" I reluctantly agreed knowing how hard this request would be for me.

As you can imagine, life would not be so easy for her in the beginning with three babies only one year apart from each other. She not only had three children of her own, she also welcomed two boys from her husband's previous marriage that were also very young. So I knew she would have many bumps and challenging roads ahead in her journey. Fortunately for me she lived close by. So therefore, being the loving and nurturing mom that I am, I stepped in on every area where I thought she needed to be rescued.

Sometimes we want to fix the problems of those close to us. We, as the boy with the butterfly, attempt to speed up a process that is under the Lord's control. We even act as if we need to fix it right now. Life changing transformations must occur in His time, and not ours. Even with the best intents, we can end up interfering with the spiritual growth of the very broken vessel we are trying to repair. It is up to the Master Designer to heal and repair. Obedience and seeking God's appointment will allow the Holy Spirit to manifest a clear vision. During our tests and trials, we learn to yield our own desires to Him; it is then we experience the righteousness of Christ. In my own life, I have experienced the touch of the Master's Hand, transforming me through a painful process of breaking and rebuilding. It was when I took the treasures I clung to so tightly, and humbly turned them over to God, that I was able to break free and walk in His eternal grace.

Chapter Ten

The Perfect Union

"Faithful Friend"

Chapter Ten:

The Perfect Union – "Faithful Friend"

"Now I beseech you brethren by the name of our Lord Jesus Christ, that ye be perfectly joined together in the same mind and in the same judgment." *(1 Cor. 1:10)*

"Every good gift and every perfect gift is from God above, and cometh down from the Father of Lights, with whom is no variations, neither shadow of turning." *(James 1:7)*

One Sunday afternoon I was on the highway driving home from the store and the Lord spoke to my heart very distinctly. He guided me to the Humane Society, which was approximately forty five minutes away. I had been there several years ago but I couldn't remember how to get there. I asked for the Lord's help and the very next thing I knew, I was pulling into my destination. When I approached the front door there was a large sign that read "CLOSED." I felt certain I was at the right place at the right time. Suddenly a woman appeared from a tent that was a covered waiting area. She asked me what I was doing there and I replied, "I was led to come here." She gasped and said "Wait here!" She then went to get her husband and the most beautiful Siberian husky I had ever seen! She said that this beautiful dog had found his way to their home. Although they could see he was special, they couldn't keep him since they already had several other dogs in their family. They made every effort to find his owner before heading to the Humane Society that Sunday. She said that she and her husband were under the tent praying that God would send the right owner for this beautiful animal. When I brought him to my car, I wept with tears of joy. What an awesome gift God had given me on that fateful day! He is and always will be a treasured member of our family.

I once had a female Siberian husky that had passed away; she is still in our hearts. I wrote this song in her honor:

My Faithful Friend

Oh my faithful friend,
We have a love that will never end

You looked up at me each and every day
In your unconditional loving way

There was nothing else that I could do

But give you back to Heaven so you could...

Roam in fields of clover
And kiss the face of God

You brought me so much joy
You would even share with me your favorite toy
You are my friend, and trusted me to the very end...

Now you roam in fields of clover
And kiss the face of God

This time with you, made me oh so glad
You even knew when I was sad

I loved to watch you run and play
Even beg, sit and stay, and most of all
Kiss my face at the end of each day...

And now you roam in fields of clover
And kiss the face of God

God brings people and pets together. Another example of a "perfect union" of pet and owner is when my friend Robert and I took another trip to the Human Society. Robert has had cats in his life for a long time. When his cat passed away years ago, his desire for another cat remained with him. One day, out of the blue, he felt compelled to go to the Humane Society to look at the cats up for adoption. He asked if I would like to go with him. I agreed to go with him, and although I am a "dog person", through Robert, I have found an admirable appreciation for this incredibly loving, yet independent creature of God's animal kingdom.

We looked at several cats and then, this one particular cat caught Robert's attention and had him brought to the adoption area. I thought, "Hmm, this cat is adopting Robert!" I thought to myself, "Well, if this cat jumps in my lap, this is definitely the one." Sure enough, right after I finished that thought, he jumped in my lap. I said to Robert, "This is the one!" Robert also has a Shiba Inu and I have the Siberian husky, so we had our dogs together when Robert brought home the cat. Both my dog and his were very curious to meet and greet the new member of the family. But the most amazing thing happened. As Robert went to put the cat up high out of the dogs reach, the cat immediately jumped down to greet the dogs. I had never seen anything like this before! The cat just gently batted his paws at the dogs when they got too close. From that first meeting forward, they have been the best of friends. Robert's reply to this unusual cat behavior: "He's just a cool customer."

Chapter Eleven

Favor

Chapter Eleven:

Favor

"A good name is rather to be chosen than great riches, and loving favor rather than silver and gold." *(Proverbs 22:1)*

God changed the names of many of His people as told in the Bible. Usually this was His way of establishing a new identity for that person. One example of this was Abram, which means "exalted father" to Abraham, which means "father of many." Abraham received a promise from God that he would have many descendants. This promise came at a time when Abraham was up in his years and his wife Sarah was barren. God's promise was fulfilled and Abraham became the father of many nations.

"No longer will you be called Abram; your name will be Abraham, for I have made you a father of many nations." (Gen. 17:5)

Back in late 1980's, I awoke one night to the sound of broken glass. I immediately went around to all of the rooms with windows and checked to see if someone had broken in. I took note of the time; it was approximately 3:00 a.m. After being relieved that all was well, I prayed, thanked God, and went back to sleep. In the morning my daughter yelled, "Mommy, come to the dining room." I ran in and found the picture that was hanging on the wall had come off the nail and was lying on the ground with the glass shattered in many pieces. Keep in mind; it had fallen on shag carpeting. I thought, "That must have been the glass I heard." After my son and daughter left for school, I called my mom who was living next door. Before I could say anything, she exclaimed, "I have to tell you that I heard glass breaking in the early hours of the morning and nothing was broken in my house!" I then asked her, "What time?" She replied, "3:00 am." I said to her that I needed to go pray and that I would call her back to explain.

I went to my room and got on my knees to pray, clearly knowing God was trying to get my attention. As I began to pray, I heard the Lord speak to me, and this is what He said, "No longer shall you be called Doris, but you shall be called Dora." Immediately I began travailing in the spirit. It was as if the death of Doris was taking place and the birth of Dora began. I was given the name Doris at birth, after my mom. My dad insisted I have this name even though he only called me "baby Dor." Before then I had never heard of the name Dora. When I gathered my composure and rose to my feet, I went to get my concordance to see if I could find the name "Dora", I found the meaning is "gift." Then I excitedly went next door to tell my mom of this glorious epiphany. She, being a believer, received the news wholeheartedly.

Other people that I had encountered did not understand right away. Ironically, it was the people in the church that I had been attending at the time who had the most trouble. What mattered to me was that all my family members were receptive even though at the time they did not quite understand it. This included my extended family too; my brothers and sisters in-law, all of whom are so very treasured and loved.

One day out of frustration, caused by some people around me, I cried out to God and said, "Lord, they are just not getting it, do I have to tell any more people about this name change?" and He spoke, "I did not say I was changing the minds of the people, I said, I changed your name." God is so gracious; He understands all of our concerns. So He inspired me to seek out the necessary information to have this done legally and I did. Although I was hesitant, God made it very clear to me that I was to share this testimony and not keep it hidden.

As my friend Robert always tells me, there is one thing to be humble and another to have false humility. Understanding our value, and being confident in who we are in Christ, is important in our walk with Him. We are made in the image of God. And He understands our needs and cares for us in ways that confounds our own understanding. We must walk with boldness so we can walk by faith and not by sight, and receive the consecration by the anointing His Holy Spirit.

Chapter Twelve

***

This is My Father's World

Chapter Twelve:

This is My Father's World

"For the Lord is coming! He will judge the world with righteousness and all nations with His truth." *(Psalm 96:13)*

———————————————— ⊙ ————————————————

One morning I awoke to birds chirping loudly with one another as if they were discussing their plans for the day. I thought, "How great and glorious is my Father's world!" This is the day the Lord has made. We will rejoice and be glad in it. (Psalm 118:23-25) So I got up and made my decision for the day. Today I will seize the day! I will not let the deceiver rob my joy today.

When we let go of all the things that try to steal us away from giving honor to the Lord; we experience a new freedom. The Father's love is so great that He gave His only Son Jesus Christ for propitiation of our sin. Therefore, every day we should give Him honor and glory in our own personal way.

I love to get up in the morning and dance before the Lord. He delights when we come before Him with thanksgiving and praise.

"And David danced before the Lord with all his might, wearing a priestly garment." (2 Samuel 6:14) Whatever your gift, use it for the glory of God. I have been studying His word a long time and I still find new revelations as I read and explore His precious word. Seek His guidance in every area of your life and you will find treasures that you never imagined were yours.

The church is the Bride of Christ which is waiting expectantly for His glorious return! Christ will return at an hour that we do not know. So therefore, God urges us to be ready at all times.

> For the Lord himself will come down from heaven with a commanding shout, with the voice of the archangel, and with the trumpet call of God. First, the Christians who have died will rise from their graves. Then, together with them, we who are still alive and remain on the earth will be caught up in the clouds to meet the Lord in the air. (1 Thessalonians 4:16-17)

How glorious will that day be when we meet Christ in the air! To forever be with Him and our loved ones.

Jesus gives us a parable in the gospel of Matthew regarding His coming.

The kingdom of Heaven will be like ten virgins who took their lamps and went to meet the bridegroom. Five of them were foolish and did not take enough oil. Five of them were wise enough to take extra oil for their lamps. When the Bridegroom was delayed, they all fell asleep. At midnight they arose with a shout "Look the Bridegroom is coming." "Come out to meet him." All the virgins got up and prepared their lamps. Then the five foolish ones asked the others, "Please give us some of your oil for our lamps are going out." But the five wise virgins replied, "We only have enough for ours, you must go and get some for yourselves." But when they left to get more oil, the bridegroom came. And those that were prepared, left with Him to the marriage feast. And the door was locked behind them. Later when the other five returned, they stood outside calling, "Lord, Lord, open the door for us!" But He called back, "Believe me, I do not know you." (Matt 25:1-13)

But we must seek the truth with a discerning spirit. We will know the true prophets of Christ by the fruit they bear:

Watch out for false prophets. They come to you in sheep's clothing, but inwardly they are ferocious wolves. By their fruit you will recognize them. Do people pick grapes from thorn bushes, or figs from thistles? Likewise every good tree bears good fruit, but a bad tree bears bad fruit. A good tree cannot bear bad fruit, and a bad tree cannot bear good fruit. Every tree that does not bear good fruit is cut down and thrown into the fire. Thus, by their fruit you will recognize them. (Matthew 15-20)

Jesus told them, "Don't let anyone mislead you, for many will come in my name, claiming, 'I am the Messiah.' They will deceive many. And you will hear of wars and threats of wars, but don't panic. Yes, these things must take place, but the end won't follow immediately. Nation will go to war against nation, and kingdom against kingdom. There will be famines and earthquakes in many parts of the world. But all this is only the first of the birth pains, with more to come." (Matthew 24:4-8).

In the news today we hear of false religions, warfare, and natural disasters. These current events are a precursor for greater trouble ahead.

Paul warned that the last days would bring an increase in false teaching. "Now the Holy Spirit tells us clearly that in the last times some will turn away from the true faith; they will follow deceptive spirits and teachings that come from demons." (1 Timothy 4:1). The last days are described as "perilous times" because of the progressively evil character of man and people who actively "oppose the truth" (2 Timothy 3:1-9; also see 2 Thessalonians 2:3). These are the characteristics of some people in the last days – "For men shall be lovers of their own selves, covetous, boasters, proud, blasphemers, disobedient to parents, unthankful, unholy" (2 Timothy 3:1-2) This is fitting of our modern age today.

> But I fear that somehow your pure and undivided devotion to Christ will be corrupted, just as Eve was deceived by the cunning ways of the serpent. You happily put up with whatever anyone tells you, even if they preach a different Jesus than the one we preach, or a different kind of Spirit than the one you received, or a different kind of gospel than the one you believed. (2 Corinthians 3-4)

By living with the expectation of His glorious coming, we are marked with His seal, signifying that we belong to Him. This does not mean that we will experience life without trials. We are sustained and strengthened during these trials by the Holy Spirit. "Anyone with ears to hear must listen to the Spirit and understand what he is saying to the churches. To everyone who is victorious I will give some of the manna that has been hidden away in heaven." (Revelation 2:17) The hidden manna is the miraculous sustenance that will be provided for our well being.

In the Gospel of Matthew, Jesus gives us a model prayer to our Father:

> Pray like this: Our Father in heaven, may your name be honored. May your Kingdom come soon. May your will be done here on earth, just as it is in heaven. Give us our food for today, and forgive us our sins, just as we have forgiven those who have sinned against us. And don't let us yield to temptation, but deliver us from the evil one.
> (Matthew 6:9-13)

This is truly our Fathers world! So, as you voyage in these perilous times, may God's Holy Spirit refresh and renew you, causing you to flourish in every province you journey.

If you have never experienced life with Christ, just bow your head right now. Admit that you have sinned against God, repent, and accept His Son Jesus as Lord and Savior of your life. Through this simple act of faith, you will be given God's precious gift of eternal salvation!

Notes

Notes

Notes

Notes

Dora Mar Books

www.doramarbooks.com